PERU
the people and culture

Bobbie Kalman & Tammy Everts

The Lands, Peoples, and Cultures Series

Toronto · Oxford · New York

Crabtree Publishing Company

The Lands, Peoples, and Cultures Series
Created by Bobbie Kalman

For my friend
Dave Rourke

Editor-in-Chief
Bobbie Kalman

Writing team
Bobbie Kalman
Tammy Everts

Editors
David Schimpky
Petrina Gentile
Lynda Hale
Janine Schaub
Tammy Everts

Consultant
Ronald Wright, author of *Cut Stones and Crossroads, A Journey in Peru* (Viking Penguin, 1984)

Computer design
Lynda Hale

Separations and film
Book Art Inc.

Printer
Worzalla Publishing Company

Special thanks to
Pierre Vachon, CIDA; Denis Nervig, Fowler Museum of Cultural History, UCLA; Federico Perez Eguren, Eco Expeditions; and Janice Emmons, World Vision

Photographs
Bonnie Bergsma: pages 13 (circle), 22 (top)
Jim Bryant: pages 5 (middle, bottom), 8 (bottom left, bottom right), 10 (bottom), 11 (all), 13 (top right), 14, 19 (right, bottom left), 23 (bottom), 25 (top left), 26, 27, 29 (bottom)
Eco Expeditions: pages 9 (bottom), 16 (bottom), 19 (top left), 26 (inset)
Pat Morrow/CIDA: pages 8 (top left), 9 (top left), 10 (circle), 20, 22 (bottom), 23 (top), 24, 25 (top right, bottom), 28, 29 (top), 30 (circle)
Denis Nervig/Fowler Museum of Cultural History: pages 4 (top), 5 (top), 17
M. Timothy O'Keefe/Tom Stack & Associates: cover, pages 13 (bottom), 15 (both)
Inga Spence/Tom Stack & Associates: page 16 (top)
Ellen Tolmie/CIDA: pages 8 (top right), 30 (bottom)
Elias Wakan/Pacific Rim Slide Bank: pages 3, 9 (top right), 21

Illustrations
Barb Bedell: title page, pages 6-7, back cover
Antoinette "Cookie" DeBiasi: page 18
Tammy Everts: page 14

The front cover shows an event from the annual Inti Raymi festival held in the city of Cusco. The golden ear ornament on the back cover is similar to those made by Moche artisans.

Published by
Crabtree Publishing Company

350 Fifth Avenue	360 York Road, RR 4,	73 Lime Walk
Suite 3308	Niagara-on-the-Lake,	Headington
New York	Ontario, Canada	Oxford OX3 7AD
N.Y. 10118	L0S 1J0	United Kingdom

Cataloging in Publication Data
Kalman, Bobbie, 1947-
  Peru: the people and culture

(Lands, Peoples, and Cultures Series)
Includes index.
ISBN 0-86505-222-0 (library bound)   ISBN 0-86505-302-2 (pbk.)
The culture and lifestyles of Peru's people are examined through their history, religion, arts, customs, occupations, and pastimes.

1. Peru - Social life and customs - Juvenile literature. 2. Peru - Civilization - Juvenile literature. 3. Peru - Social conditions - Juvenile literature. I. Everts, Tammy, 1970-   . II. Title. III. Series.

F3408.5.K35 1994   j985   LC 94-885

Contents

Ancient cultures

People have lived in what is now Peru for at least 12,000 years. Archaeologists believe that the first communities were located on the coast. The inhabitants of these early villages depended on fishing and farming for food. Over the centuries, several **civilizations** emerged in Peru. Civilizations are societies that are accomplished in arts and sciences.

The Chavín civilization

The Chavín civilization existed from 900 BC to 200 BC. The Chavín developed skills such as carving, embroidery, and pottery-making. Their religious beliefs centered around the powers of nature. Snakes, jaguars, and birds of prey were important objects of worship. The ruins of a large Chavín temple, filled with underground tunnels, can be found north of Lima in the town of Chavín de Huántar.

The Nascas

The Nascas were named after the Nasca Valley in which they lived. They also inhabited the Paracas Peninsula on the southwestern coast of Peru. The Nascas were most powerful between 200 BC and AD 500. Scientists believe that these ancient people knew more about astronomy and mathematics than the Chavín. Nasca arts and crafts were also more elaborate than those of the Chavín. The Nascas made ceramic pots that were decorated with many colors. Over time, Nasca textiles developed from simple embroidery to complicated woven tapestries.

The mysterious Moche

Between AD 100 and 800, the Moche became a powerful civilization in Peru. The Moche were accomplished farmers. They had irrigation systems for growing corn, beans, squash, peanuts, and potatoes in the dry coastal regions. They were also skilled artisans and architects. Their pyramids were towering structures made of adobe brick. The Moche worshiped the forces

This brightly painted Nasca pot is between 1500 and 2000 years old. **Archaeologists** *find and study artifacts in order to learn about the past.*

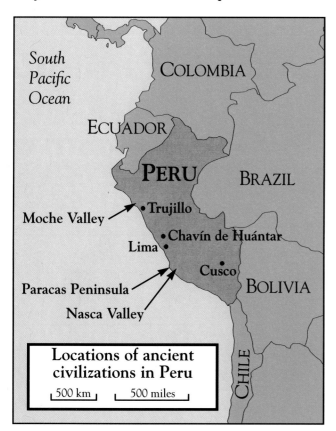

South Pacific Ocean

COLOMBIA

ECUADOR

PERU

BRAZIL

Moche Valley — • Trujillo

• Chavín de Huántar

Lima •

Cusco •

Paracas Peninsula

BOLIVIA

Nasca Valley

CHILE

Locations of ancient civilizations in Peru

500 km   500 miles

of nature. There are many scenes of warfare in Moche art, and their beautifully crafted pottery shows almost every aspect of daily life.

The Chimú culture

The Chimú developed from the Moche civilization and thrived between AD 1000 and 1470. The Chimú were skilled potters, weavers, and metalworkers. They were responsible for building the huge walled city of Chan Chan, which is still standing. The Chimú were eventually conquered by the Incas.

The powerful Incas

The Incas lived in the Cusco region of Peru as early as the 1100s, but historians have recorded 1438 as the beginning of their empire. From 1438 to 1532, the Incas expanded their empire across Peru. They were conquered by the Spanish in 1532. The Incas were the most powerful Native group in Peru for less than one hundred years, but they made a lasting impression in that short period.

Spaniards, slaves, and laborers

When the Spanish came, they took over much of Peru's farmlands and resources of gold and silver. They forced many Native peoples to work on the farms and in the mines. The Europeans also brought African slaves and, later, Asian laborers to Peru. Millions of people died in the Spaniards' silver mines, and most farm workers were treated poorly. In the middle of the nineteenth century the slaves were freed, and the workers found better jobs. Although conditions have improved in modern times, life is still hard for many Peruvians.

(top) Moche "stirrup-spout" bottles have handles that also serve as drinking or pouring spouts.
(center) The dry climate of the coastal region has helped preserve the ancient Chimú capital of Chan Chan, which is located near the modern city of Trujillo.
(bottom) The Native peoples of Peru are descendants of the peoples of ancient civilizations.

The Inca empire

Who were the Incas?

Originally, "Inca" was the family name of the rulers who lived in the city of Cusco, high in the Andes Mountains. Later, many Native people who learned Inca ways and rose to a high position in the empire were called "Incas." When the Spaniards arrived, they called all the Native peoples in the Inca empire "Indians." The ruler was called "Sapa Inca."

The Sapa Inca

The title "Sapa Inca" meant "only emperor." The Sapa Inca's subjects believed that this ruler was god on earth because he was descended from the Sun God, Inti. The Sapa Inca's word was law. No ordinary woman was considered good enough to be his queen, so the Sapa Inca had to marry the eldest of his sisters, who was another descendant of the Sun God. She was called the Coya. The Sapa Inca also had over one hundred "secondary wives."

Religious beliefs

The Incas believed in gods who represented the different parts of nature. The most important natural god was the Sun God, Inti. Every major Inca city had a large carved stone, called an Intihuatana, that marked the days on which the sun passed directly overhead at noon. On these days, festivals of chanting, drinking, and singing were held to thank Inti for providing warmth and light. Llamas, guinea pigs and, occasionally, humans were sacrificed to the Sun God.

Viracocha, the Creator, ruled over the gods. He was often pictured as a human or as an oval, which represented the universe. Some legends said that he had left the earth but would one day return.

The Incas believed that certain places and objects were inhabited by supernatural forces. These holy sites, called *huacas*, included temples, tombs, hills, natural springs, and caves. Some spirits were also thought to live in plants. Inca healers used herbs to treat the sick. They attributed their cures to the plant spirits.

Keeping records

The Incas had no written system for recording information. Instead, they used a *quipu*, which was a network of different-colored strings. The colors of the strings and the number and position of knots along the strings recorded the goods and people in each city. The Inca accountant or historian who kept track of the quipu was called a *quipucamayoc*.

Giving and receiving

Inca society was based on sharing. People did not work for money. The goods they produced were distributed as people needed them. Young married couples received a house and some land for farming. For each child born, the couple was given more land. Children helped in the fields and at home. Older people were given simple tasks such as collecting firewood and teaching the children. After a lifetime of working, elderly Incas were not required to earn their keep. The state provided them with food and clothing.

Farmers worked on the terraced land that was located outside the cities. Nobles and rulers lived in the Inca cities. The Sapa Inca traveled throughout his empire on a litter carried by his servants. Regular citizens used llamas for traveling and carrying heavy loads. Suspension bridges, which required great skill to build, enabled travelers to cross deep gorges.

🦙 The people of Peru 🦙

Many different cultures exist in Peru. About half the population is made up of Native people who speak either Quechua, the language of the Incas, or Aymara. Most Native people live in the Andes Mountains. Smaller Native groups, such as the Mayoruna, live in the tropical rainforest and have little contact with the outside world. At least one-third of Peruvians are of mixed Native and Spanish heritage. These people are called *mestizos*. People of European descent, or *criollos*, make up about a tenth of Peru's population. There are smaller groups of people who are of African and Asian origin.

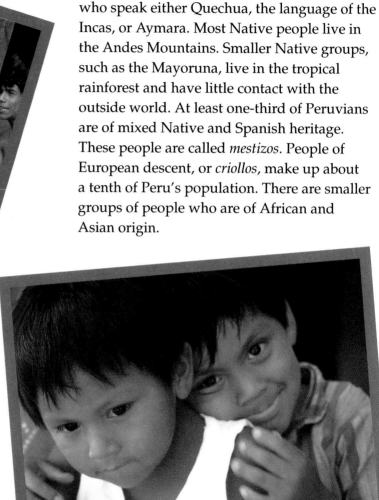

The Urus of Lake Titicaca

Guidebooks urge tourists to visit the Uru people on the "floating islands" of Lake Titicaca. The modern islanders, however, are not true Urus—they are mainland Aymaras who have adopted the Uru way of life. For hundreds of years the Urus kept their own customs despite Inca and Spanish invasions, but the last of the true Urus died over 30 years ago.

The floating islands are made of thick layers of reeds. Reeds are also the main material in houses, sleeping mats, baskets, and boats. They are even eaten! Traditional reed canoes take hours to make, but they last for months. The boats are used for fishing, as well as for hunting frogs and ducks. Modern reed boats have a foam core—an addition that makes the boats more buoyant.

🦙 A variety of homes 🦙

Peruvians live in a variety of homes. In the cities, the wealthy inhabit modern homes or old mansions that were built when Peru was a Spanish colony. Others rent or own apartments in high-rise buildings. Most city dwellers, however, cannot afford such comfortable homes. They live in simple shacks made of building materials such as discarded cardboard, wood, tin, or stones. Neighbors often help one another build their homes. (See also photographs on page 29.)

In rural areas, homes are designed to protect their inhabitants from the environment. For example, sturdy mountain homes provide shelter from winds and cold temperatures. In the rainforest, houses built on poles keep their occupants dry when heavy rains flood the land.

(circle) In the rainforest, many families often share one large house. The houses are built atop supports to keep them from being flooded during heavy rains. The floors and supports are made of hardwoods that discourage hungry insects from chewing through. On hot days, cool breezes blow through the window spaces.
(bottom) In the mountains of Peru, rural homes are sturdy. They are constructed with stones or adobe bricks. The roofs are made of straw or grass.

(top) The floating homes in this fishing community are built on rafts. They have straw roofs and walls made of planks.
(bottom right) Desert homes are constructed of materials such as clay, straw, and stones. Frequent earthquakes make building with heavy, collapsible materials dangerous.
(bottom left) The Native people of Lake Titicaca use the plentiful local reeds to "weave" their homes.

Peruvians are free to practice the religion of their choice. Most Peruvians, however, are Roman Catholic. The Spanish brought the Catholic religion to Peru in the 1500s and forced many of the Native peoples to adopt this faith. Today, most Native peoples blend their ancient customs and traditions with Catholic beliefs. Peruvians celebrate their religious heritage with lively festivals called **fiestas**.

The Feast of Corpus Christi

One important festival in the mountain region occurs every year at the end of June. During the Feast of Corpus Christi, people from surrounding areas come to the city of Cusco for eight days. Statues of saints, which are housed in the churches of Cusco, are honored and dressed in beautiful costumes. On the eighth day of the festival a procession is held. Musicians, dancers, and other participants parade through the city streets. The Feast of Corpus Christi is around the same time of year as Inti Raymi. Inti Raymi is an ancient Inca sun-worshiping festival that celebrates the middle of Peru's winter and the end of the harvest. It is held on June 24.

Star of the Snow Festival

The Native people living in the Cusco region gather every year for Qoyllur Riti, or Star of the Snow. This ancient festival, which is also held near the end of June, celebrates the snow of the mountain glaciers. It also recalls a miracle—the appearance of Jesus Christ to a farmer nearly two centuries ago. During Star of the Snow, many people make a pilgrimage to a glacier high in the mountains. When the climbers reach the glacier, they pray and cut chunks of ice, which they carry home. This ice is believed to have healing powers.

Our Lord of Miracles

October is springtime in Peru! Every October in the city of Huancayo, the procession of Our Lord of Miracles takes place. People honor a gold-framed portrait of Jesus Christ. The picture is a copy of a painting found on a wall that was left standing when an earthquake destroyed the surrounding buildings in 1746. This festival also celebrates the beginning of the growing season. By honoring Jesus Christ, people hope to be rewarded with good crops.

La Fiesta de Sanchocay

Every January, a farming community called Huayacuchi celebrates La Fiesta de Sanchocay. A highlight of the festival is a fight between a *gamonal* and a *chinchilpa*. The *gamonal* is dressed in blue. He stands for the "evil" landlords. Everyone cheers for the *chinchilpa*, who wears a red costume. He represents the farmers, or *campesinos*. The two fight one another with whips for about 30 seconds. If the *chinchilpa* wins, the people believe that they will enjoy a bountiful harvest.

Mountain worship

The Incas built mountaintop sites to worship the sun and mountains. They honored the sun because it provided them with warmth and light. The mountains were important because their high peaks seemed to touch the sun. Today, Native people continue to honor the mountains. Before beginning a journey through the Andes, travelers make offerings of statues, coca leaves, incense, and llama fat. These offerings are sold in the village markets in bundles called *despachos*.

Jungle magic

Some Native groups in the rainforest believe in the powers of **shamans**. These sorcerers use the bark of a vine to brew a potion called *ayahuasca*. After drinking it, they believe they can travel in space or time and transform themselves into animals such as jaguars and anacondas. Some shamans and *curanderos* (healers) cast bad spells, but most use their powers for healing and protecting people.

(right) Statues of Christian figures such as Mary and Jesus are located throughout Peru. They are evidence that most Peruvians belong to the Roman Catholic faith.

(circle) At La Fiesta de Sanchocay, a **chinchilpa** *and a* **gamonal** *fight to predict the success of the year's crops.*

(bottom) During the Inti Raymi festival, brightly costumed performers dance and offer gifts of food to Inti, the Sun God, in thanks for the warmth and light he provides.

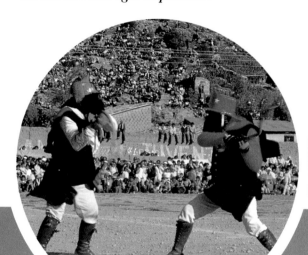

Music and dance

Music and dance were an essential part of life for the ancient Incas. Today, music and dance are still important in Peru. They make the country's many celebrations even more festive. There are two main musical styles: coastal (*criolla*) and highland (*andina*). Coastal music tends to be energetic and merry, whereas highland music is often slow and mournful. Peruvian music varies from region to region, but flutes, harps, and violins are almost always a part of the sound.

Inca instruments

Throughout the mountain region of Peru, music of Inca origin is still popular. Age-old melodies are produced using traditional Native instruments. The *quena*, which is like a flute, is often made from an animal bone. Several pipes of different sizes make up the *antara*. The *bombo leguero* is a huge drum constructed of willow and goat skin. A *charango* is like a small guitar with one difference—the body of the *charango* is made from the shell of an armadillo!

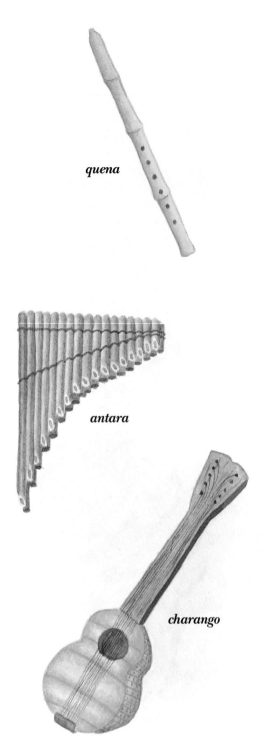

quena

antara

charango

(top) Native Peruvians have played the **quena** for over 2000 years. Traditionally, only men were allowed to play this flutelike instrument.
(center) The **antara**, too, was only played by men. **Antaras** can be made of clay, bone, wood, or even the quills of large birds.
(bottom) The guitarlike **charango** usually has ten strings.
(right) Many Peruvian street musicians are blind. Playing music is a way for them to make money.

14

Dance of the coast

The *marinera* is a dance that is performed at fiestas in the coastal region of Peru. Guitar strumming and lively singing provide background music for a pretend courtship, which is acted out by couples waving colored handkerchiefs.

Mountain dancing

Over 200 different dances are performed by the Native peoples in the mountain region. The *huaynito serrano* is one. It is a type of walking dance with slow, skipping steps that are repeated over and over. This sad-looking dance is accompanied by the music of a harp and a *quena*.

Dancers of Los Panchitos

The Los Panchitos dance troupe travels around Peru and performs at festivals. The dancers act out **morality plays**, which poke fun at human faults. Although the Los Panchitos dances are performed during Christian festivals, they originated long before Christianity came to South America.

(right and below) Dancers clad in colorful costumes perform traditional Native dances during religious festivals in the mountains.

(above) Modern artist Juan Lozavo captures Peru's Native heritage in his colorful murals.

(below) The magnificent ruins of Machu Picchu attract thousands of fascinated visitors each year.

🦙 An artistic heritage 🦙

Peruvian artists and craftsworkers have had many influences. Spanish and modern art forms have inspired some artisans, but most look to Peru's rich Native heritage. Peruvian folk art is popular around the world, but Peru is especially famous for the amazing buildings that were constructed by its ancient peoples.

Pyramid of the Sun

The largest existing Moche pyramid is the Huaca del Sol, or Pyramid of the Sun, which is located near the city of Trujillo. Standing 45 meters (147 feet) high, the pyramid occupies 5 hectares (12 acres) of land. Over 140 million adobe bricks were used to construct the walls. So much mud was needed to make the bricks that a nearby pit from which the mud was scooped has become a permanent lake! When the Spaniards arrived in South America, Huaca del Sol was one of the largest structures in the New World.

Machu Picchu

The archaeologist Hiram Bingham described the ruins of Machu Picchu as "the Great Pyramid and the Grand Canyon rolled into one." This beautiful ancient city was built in a cradle of mountain peaks. The ruins are surrounded by terraces, which were used as fields for growing food. Machu Picchu is one of the few Inca cities that were never found or damaged by the Spaniards. This fabulous city is complete except for the roofs of its many buildings. Today, people visit Machu Picchu by train or by walking along an ancient Inca road through the mountains.

Native pride

An artistic and literary movement called Indigenism became popular in the 1920s. Led by a woodcarver named José Sabogal, Indigenism celebrates the culture and heritage of Peru's Native peoples. The most famous Indigenist artist was a man named Jorge Vihatea Reynoso. Sculptors, writers, wall artists called **muralists**, and other artists all use their talents to express their Native pride.

Folk arts

Many of the folk arts created in modern Peru are made using skills that have been passed down for generations. Craftspeople living in the town of Mórrope mold clay pots and "stirrup-spout" bottles very similar to those made by the ancient Moche. Native peoples living in the Cusco region weave colorful textiles much like those woven by the Incas.

Women living in the shantytowns around large cities stitch *arpilleras* to sell to tourists. These appliquéd pictures of everyday life allow women to earn money to help provide food and shelter for their families. Visitors to Peru can buy a hard-shelled fruit, called a **gourd**, which has been dried and engraved with intricate designs. This craft is called a *mate burilado*.

(above) This Nasca effigy jar represents a ruler or other important person. Modern Native craftsworkers use methods and traditions passed down from their ancestors.

🦙 Peruvian clothing 🦙

The Native arts of weaving and dyeing fabric have been passed down from generation to generation for hundreds of years. These arts are still used in making traditional Native clothing. Colonial Spanish clothing has also influenced Peruvian fashions. Although most people wear modern clothing in their daily lives, traditional Native and Spanish costumes are often worn at festivals and on other special occasions.

Native clothing

The Quechua-speaking people are the largest Native group in Peru. Quechua girls and women wear several layers of long, handwoven skirts. These skirts are usually black, but they are decorated with bright, colorful trimming. A short cape, or *liclla*, is wrapped around the shoulders or draped over the head.

Native men wear a shirt, vest, or coat over their calf-length or full-length black trousers. A brightly colored sash is sometimes knotted at the waist. In the mountain region, a **poncho** or *serape* provides necessary warmth on chilly nights. The poncho is pulled over the head, whereas the *serape* opens at the front, like a jacket.

Costume of the *caballero*

The man and woman on this page are dressed in traditional Spanish-colonial clothing. Some Peruvians still put on these costumes for special occasions. The man is wearing a *caballero*, or cowboy, outfit. His short velvet jacket, called a *bolero*, is worn over a fine white shirt made of silk or satin. Tight velvet breeches match the *bolero*. *Chaparajos*, or "chaps," which go over the breeches, are ornamented with fancy white and black braid. A black felt hat and black leather boots complete this eye-catching costume.

The woman is dressed in the same type of clothing that might have been worn by a fine Spanish lady hundreds of years ago. She wears an embroidered fringed shawl over a white satin gown. A lace *mantilla* is draped over her hair and held in place by a fancy comb.

(top) Many people in Native mountain communities wear traditional "pancake" hats embroidered with colorful yarn. People sometimes put a tight knitted cap called a chullo on under their pancake hat.

(bottom) Some Native girls and women drape a short shawl called a lliclla over their hair. On cold days, they wear a hat over the lliclla.

(right) This girl is wearing a combination of traditional and non-traditional clothing. Layers of embroidered skirts and a colorful vest contrast with modern track pants and running shoes. A traditional pouch worn at the waist holds spinning tools and wool.

🦙 A taste of Peru 🦙

Peruvian cuisine is a multicultural blend of Native, African, European, and Asian dishes. In rural areas, Native people enjoy traditional foods. Peru's cities offer a cosmopolitan blend of foods and drinks. Chinese and Japanese restaurants can be found everywhere, serving traditional *chow meins* and *sushi*. Other restaurants feature tempting meals such as a grilled chicken dish called *chicharrones de pollo* and *pachamanca*— a hearty stew cooked over heated stones.

Regional cuisine

Most Peruvian meals include rice, beans, fish, tomatoes, and spicy red and yellow peppers, but foods differ from region to region. Raw fish seasoned with lemon and vinegar, called *cebiche*, is popular along the coast. Potatoes, onions, beans, garlic, and sweet potatoes called *camotes* are eaten regularly in the mountains. Grains such as barley, oats, and *quinoa* are essential for daily cooking. The people of the mountain region also enjoy salted beef, mutton, and llama meat.

Rainforest food

The Native peoples of the rainforest hunt and eat a wide variety of animals, such as tapirs, wild pigs, rabbits, and monkeys. Doves, partridges, and wild turkeys provide poultry meat. A dry salted fish called *paiche* is a popular dish. Tree sap is a light, refreshing drink. *Masato* and *canazo* are alcoholic beverages made from fermented plants and fruits.

Corn beer

Chicha is a Peruvian corn beer that has been brewed since ancient times. The Incas drank *chicha* during religious festivals. Today, people enjoy it any day of the year. *Chicha* tastes bitter when fermented. Unfermented, it is a delicious, non-alcoholic beverage. Businesses that specialize in brewing *chicha* have red flags hanging over their doors.

Chicha *vendors sell this centuries-old beverage on the streets of Cusco. The Incas drank* **chicha** *from specially painted or engraved beakers called* **keros.**

Natillas piuranas

This very sweet milk pudding is a favorite dessert in Peru and other Latin American countries. It has many names, such as *manjar blanco*, *dulce de leche*, and *leche quemada*. This recipe serves six to eight people. Ask an adult for help when using the stove.

750 ml (3 cups) milk
450 ml (1 3/4 cups) condensed milk
2.5 ml (1/2 tsp) baking soda
250 ml (1 cup) dark-brown sugar
60 ml (1/4 cup) water

In a small saucepan over high heat, bring the milk, condensed milk, and baking soda to a boil, while stirring constantly. Remove pan from heat. Combine the sugar and water in a large, heavy saucepan and cook over low heat, stirring until the sugar dissolves. Add the hot milk mixture and stir well. Cook over low heat for 75 minutes. Stir occasionally. The mixture will become a thick, amber-colored pudding. Serve at room temperature or refrigerate and serve chilled. To add color and flavor, you can sprinkle the pudding lightly with cinnamon.

(above) Farmers work together on cooperative farms that produce crops and livestock.

(below) Painting and selling their work on city streets is good business for artists who cannot afford to open a gallery.

The working world

Peruvians have the same types of jobs as those of people in other countries. Some work close to the land and sea as farmers and fishers; others attend many years of school to become doctors and teachers. Singers, shopkeepers, secretaries, and scientists each play an important role in the country's workforce.

Employment problems

Peru's cities are crowded with people who are looking for work. Unfortunately, only a few will find jobs. Many people are unemployed and live in poverty; others have jobs but receive very low pay for their work. Peru's government does not have enough money to help all the people who are unemployed or underpaid. Some people hope that foreign companies will create jobs by building businesses and factories in Peru. Others worry that foreigners may take more out of Peru than they bring in.

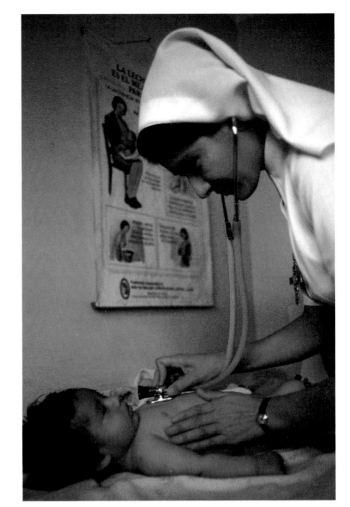

(above) Some doctors and nurses work in clinics. This clinic specializes in caring for mothers and babies.
(left) Teachers face the challenge of overcrowded schools. A group of students takes a break from work to learn a traditional dance.

Peruvians work hard, but when they have some spare time, they like to play hard, too! Some sports, such as *fútbol* and bullfighting, were brought to Peru by the Spanish. Newer games have been "borrowed" from the United States and other parts of the world.

Fútbol

The most popular sport in Peru is *fútbol*, or soccer. The National Stadium, or Estadio Nacional, where *fútbol* is played, is always crowded during games. Every four years, countries around the world compete in the World Cup Games to determine the international *fútbol* champions. Peruvians watch the games enthusiastically, especially if a team from Peru is playing!

Fighting the bulls

Bullfighting was introduced to Peru by the Spanish conquerors in the sixteenth century. A bullfighter, or *torero*, in a tight costume swirls a red cape around his or her shoulders. The movement of the cape enrages the bull into charging at the bullfighter, who leaps gracefully from the bull's path just in time to escape its horns. Eventually, the bull is killed because it is too tired to fight. Some people consider bullfighting a cruel sport, whereas others think it is like watching a beautiful dance. Bullfighting fans from

as far away as Spain visit the Plaza de Acho in the city of Lima. It is the largest bullring in South America.

Cockfights

Cockfighting is illegal in many countries, but it is very popular in Peru. Some people bet on the outcome of the cockfights. Specially trained roosters called *peleadores* wear sharp, curved blades on their feet. While the spectators cheer, the roosters fight and slash at one another until one is dead. The Coliseo de Gallos Sandia is the most popular cockfighting arena in Peru. People who wish to see "gentler" cockfighting can go to the Gallo de Oro, where the roosters fight only with their beaks.

Enjoying nature

Peruvians who can afford to travel take advantage of the natural beauty of their country. Hikers and mountain climbers are drawn to the breathtaking mountain landscapes of the Andes. Some vacationers enjoy visiting the scenic villages along Peru's coast. City dwellers who cannot afford to travel long distances take a break from the bustle of the inner city and flock to the beautiful beaches of the coast.

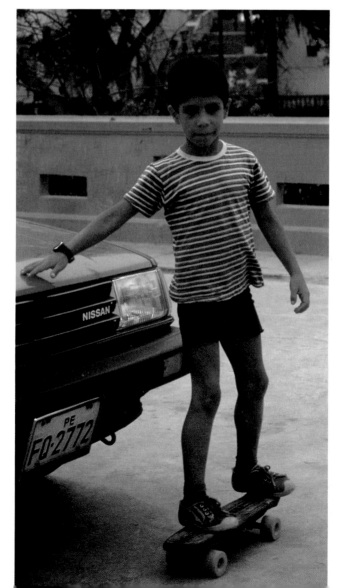

(left) Skateboarding is a favorite pastime for many young Peruvians.

(above) **Fútbol** *is the national sport of Peru. Professional teams play it in the stadiums; young people play it in the schoolyards just for fun!*
(right) *Playing volleyball is a great way for Peruvians to stay in shape!*
(below) *Peruvians can enjoy the wonders of nature by visiting bird sanctuaries.*

🦙 Rural life 🦙

Most of the Native peoples in the mountain region work as farmers, just as their ancestors did. Some farmers, however, grow unhappy with their simple lifestyle and move to the cities. Facing poverty and overcrowding in the city, many soon come to regret leaving the countryside. Other families live contentedly in their rural homes and carry on the customs and traditions of their Native ancestors.

José's farm

José is twelve years old. He and his family live on their farm outside the city of Cusco, high in the Andes Mountains. They are Quechuas, descendants of the Incas.

Every morning, José's family awakens at dawn to begin a long day of work. José and his father spend the day working in the fields. As José straightens up from hoeing to stretch his back, he notices his father gazing proudly at the rows of corn, beans, and squash. José's father is happy because harvest time is approaching, and it looks as if this year's crops will be bountiful. The farm is small, but it produces enough food for the family and a little extra to sell at the market.

While José and his father work in the fields, his mother and ten-year-old sister, Luisa, are busy in the simple, one-room house. Together they grind dried corn for cooking. They hoe and weed in the small garden near the house, where onions and sweet potatoes grow. Anna—the baby of the family—rides in a shawl on her mother's back, where she is safe and out of the way.

In the afternoon, Luisa and her mother weave with their backstrap looms. They make all the cloth for the family's clothes. The cloth comes from llama and alpaca wool. When she was very young, Luisa learned to weave from her mother, who learned it from Luisa's grandmother. Luisa's mother tells her that the patterns their people create have been passed down from generation to generation for hundreds—perhaps even thousands—of years. Luisa finds it hard to believe that the designs can be so old, but she knows that her mother is a wise woman.

After dinner that evening, José and Luisa play outside. Shortly after the sun sets, it is time for bed. Tired from his day's work, José falls asleep listening to the soft breathing of his parents and sisters.

(above) José wears a wool **chullo** *to keep his head warm.*
(opposite page) José, his mother, and his two sisters walk to the local well to bring back drinking water.
(opposite page, inset) The family llama carries goods to the market, and José's mother carries baby Anna.

🦙 Living in the city 🦙

Over 70 percent of Peru's population lives in the busy cities. Peru's cities are exciting places filled with beautiful buildings, fascinating museums, wonderful shops, and flower-filled parks. Unfortunately, many cities, such as Lima, are troubled by crime, poverty, and overcrowding. For those who can afford to live in a good home, life is comfortable. There are many others, however, who live in unsanitary, overcrowded conditions. For these people, life is a daily struggle.

María in Miraflores

Twelve-year-old María lives in a large, beautiful house in the Miraflores suburb of Lima. Every day she goes to a private school, which is run by the Roman Catholic church. Today María is excited because her older brother Javier is visiting. Javier attends university on the other side of the city, so he must live away from home.

He has promised María that he will walk her to school this morning. María is proud to be seen with her smart, handsome brother.

At school, María enjoys most of her lessons. She learns math, science, geography, history, art, and music. María also studies English. Someday she would like to travel around the world, and she thinks knowing English will be useful. Science is María's favorite subject. Her brother's major subject is history, but María would like to study science when she goes to university. She wants to be a doctor—or maybe an astronaut!

For now, though, María enjoys being young and playing with her friends. After school she invites her best friends, Federico and Anna, to her house. They play in her back yard until María's mother calls her inside. María has forgotten that they are supposed to go shopping. Her confirmation is approaching, and she needs a long fancy dress. María does not really care for dresses, but she loves to visit the modern Camino Real Shopping Center with her mother.

Dinner that evening turns out to be a special treat—hamburgers! María's mother prefers to have her family eat traditional Peruvian foods such as corn, beans, rice, and seafood, but she sometimes makes an exception for her children, who love "American" food. After dinner the family goes for a walk in the nearby park and then returns home to watch some television before going to bed.

Fernando in the *barriada*

Fernando is twelve. He lives in a different part of Lima: the *barriada*. The *barriada* is a shantytown filled with thousands of one-room shacks. These run-down shacks have no indoor plumbing or electricity. Many of the people who live in the *barriada* are unemployed and suffer terrible poverty. The government tries to pretend that the shantytowns are acceptable places to live by calling them *pueblos jóvenes*, or "young towns."

Fernando is luckier than the many children who live in the streets and have no families at all. At least he has parents and a roof over his head! His father manages to make a little money working as a street vendor, or *ambulante*. He sells handmade jewelry to tourists in downtown Lima. Fernando's mother stays home and takes care of the younger children. Fernando's parents would like to send him to school, but there are no schools in the shantytown. Instead, Fernando, like his father, must work as a street vendor to help support his family.

This morning Fernando wakes up early to begin another long day of work. He is very hungry, but there is only boiled rice and water for breakfast. Fernando does not complain, for he knows that everyone else is just as hungry as he is. The rest of the family waves goodbye as Fernando and his father leave for another working day.

(above) Beautiful mansions line the streets of the Miraflores suburb in Lima, where María lives. (below) Crime and unsanitary conditions are two serious problems in Peru's many shantytowns, or **barriadas.** *The* **barriada** *in which Fernando lives has no electricity, sewers, schools, or hospitals.*

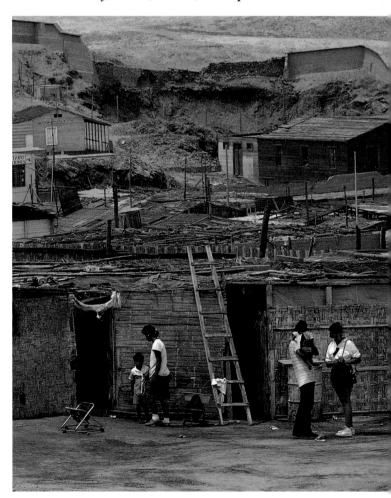

29

Fernando's long day

Some days Fernando sells newspapers. Today he walks around with a bucket of soapy water and a rag, offering to wash cars. Some people pay him a few coins for his work. People often ignore him or treat him rudely, but Fernando tries not to let this bother him.

At the end of the day, Fernando meets his father and they return home. Both are happy because they have made a bit more money than usual. Fernando's mother has cooked beans and rice for dinner. After their small meal, the children play with some other children in their neighborhood. Soon it is time for bed.

As he lies in his bed on the floor, Fernando listens to his mother and father talk. Many years ago, they came to Lima from their village in the mountains to find jobs and better lives. Unfortunately, there were not enough jobs for the millions of people who had the same idea.

Now they cannot afford the long trip home and are forced to live in the *barriada*. Fernando's parents worry about the growing crime and poverty in Lima, but they are filled with hope for the future. They are saving money so they can return to the mountains and become farmers again. That night, Fernando dreams of the mountains that were once his home.

(circle) Selling newspapers is one way for Fernando to make money. Many children must work to help support their families.
(bottom) Charitable organizations have meal programs to feed children who do not get enough to eat.

ꙮ Glossary ꙮ

accountant A person who records and sorts financial facts and figures

adobe Clay or soil that can be shaped into bricks and dried in the sun

alpaca A South American animal related to the camel and llama

anaconda A large tropical snake

Andes Mountains A large mountain range in western South America

appliqué A decoration or ornament made by cutting pieces of one fabric and sewing them onto the surface of another fabric

armadillo A small burrowing animal, found in South America and parts of North America, whose body is protected by an armor of bony plates

artisan A person skilled in a craft

astronomy The study of the stars and planets

backstrap loom A weaving device that requires the weaver to lean forward and backward to control the loom's movement

beaker A large, open glass or pot

breeches Knee-length pants

buoyant Describing something that floats on water

ceramic A type of glazed pottery

chow mein A thick stew of shredded meat, mushrooms, vegetables, and seasonings served with fried noodles

coastal region A dry part of Peru that lies between the Andes Mountains and the Pacific Ocean

coca A type of South American shrub. Dried coca leaves are chewed by the Native peoples of Peru and used to make tea. The leaves can also be made into an illegal and dangerous drug called cocaine.

colony A group of settlers in a new country who are still ruled by their home country

confirmation A Christian ceremony in which a person renews his or her faith and is given full membership in the church

cosmopolitan Describing the many cultures and lifestyles that can exist in a large city

effigy An item, such as a statue or doll, meant to resemble a certain person

embroidery The art of decorating cloth with fancy needlework

empire A group of countries or territories having the same ruler or government

fermentation The chemical change in a liquid that can make it alcoholic

folk art Crafts that originate among the common people of a region or country

gorge A narrow opening between hills

incense A substance that produces a fragrant odor when burned

irrigate To supply land with water by means of channels, streams, or pipes

Latin America The Spanish- and Portuguese-speaking countries south of the United States

litter A stretcher carried by men or animals

llama A South American animal related to the camel

mutton The meat from a sheep

New World The name given to North and South America by sixteenth-century explorers

peninsula A strip of land that juts into a body of water

pilgrimage A journey made for religious reasons

procession A group of persons or vehicles moving along in an orderly, formal manner

rainforest A dense forest in an area of heavy rainfall

Roman Catholic Describing or relating to the organization of Christians headed by the Pope

rural Describing something in the country

shantytown A community in which the homes are simple shacks

sorcerer A magician or wizard

suburb A residential area outside a city

supernatural Describing powers outside the forces of nature

sushi A Japanese dish of prepared raw fish

suspension bridge A bridge suspended from ropes or cables hung between towers or posts

tapestry A heavy cloth with pictures woven into it

tapir A large piglike animal that sleeps during the day and is active at night

terrace A platform along a steep slope that is used as farmland

textile Woven cloth

troupe A company of dancers, actors, or acrobats

♦ Index ♦

2 3 4 5 6 7 8 9 0 Printed in the U.S.A. 3 2 1 0 9 8 7 6 5 4